Everyday Spirituality

Joseph Raffa

Everyday Spirituality

Author: Joseph Raffa

Editor: Teena Raffa-Mulligan

ISBN 978-0-9944990-4-2

eISBN 978-0-9944990-7-3

Author's note: The term 'mankind' as used throughout this discourse is a reference to the human race collectively.

Published by Sea Song Publications

sea-song@bigpond.com

www.seasongpublications.com

CONTENTS

1

PRACTICAL SPIRITUALITY

WHAT is it that signifies a spiritually awakened person? Can it be recognised from the outer or is the certainty of it something experienced inwardly? Is it related to healing, to insights into the future, into past lives, or are the unusual manifestations that happen from time to time just by-products, useful in a way but not that important apart from the healing of sickness which is always welcome?

There is an inner healing, a making whole that signals an awakening spirituality. This healing is of a very special kind. It irradiates the total person. Every aspect is touched in some way — mental, emotional and physical. It results from a moment of integration. Diversity ends and one-ness reigns. All the divergent aspects of the personality are brought together in a unified whole.

So much has been written of the need to return to our universal source. Many are the sacred texts left by past masters who walked the public stage giving freely of their understanding and love to those eager to share this unusual bounty from beyond the mind.

What they conveyed was the reality they had discovered. Those who listened to the words and not the true meaning made of it what they would. Today, the gulf between words and realisation remains as wide as ever.

Everyone has access to the words. Everyone has access to what was being conveyed from beyond the words. But the self has a limited vision and when it listens and acts from this, it stays there. Words then, become a playground, something to interpret, to speculate over, even to argue about. What they truly represent is ignored — unrealised — so wholeness doesn't get a chance to show its transforming power.

Herein lies the true significance of spirituality — the moment to moment putting aside of the self that thrives on words, on images, feelings and sensations. While the self holds the centre stage with its busy antics, all the characteristics of the self come to life. So too, do the divisions and the sense of separation that the self is imbued with in its dealings with body, thoughts, feelings and the outer world.

In those who have integrated with wholeness, this familiar process continues. Inwardly, the illusion of separation has been discarded as the truthful view of what is taking place. They have left the limited and the known to lodge in the unlimited and the unknown. This brings the surface self under the control of a higher directive. The former power to act for and by itself is minimised, even at times put aside as the call goes out from a higher level to allow aspects of a spiritual expression to come through without interruption.

In lives lacking spiritual lustre, the unusual manifestations that surface from time to time are considered of greater significance. They are the highlights that brighten up an otherwise drab and boring life devoid of self-discovery.

When lives are empty of true meaning, when the limited self has not been uplifted by a universal input, exaggerated importance is given to the unusual features that surface. The focus is not on the *what is*, on the source, but on a lower level of existence.

Just like the astronauts who journeyed to the moon have a first-hand knowledge others do not have, so spiritual discoverers have a deeper and wider awareness of the living process. They may not have the technical knowledge of those versed in the direction of facts and techniques but their adventurous explorations have taken them inwards towards the Silent Heart of *what is*.

On the way, much has unfolded that is surprising and unusual but with this they do not rest content. Their hearts are set on integration with the universal, so the resting places of experience, even the remarkable, are just momentary pauses as onwards they go, eager to merge completely with the heart's desire.

The story that unfolds is not only a private one but also a universal one — not only a present one but also a historical one. The inner contains the records of mankind's and the universal movements. Glimpses of these come to light along the way. Not that every facet yields its mystery by any means but enough to show what we come from, what we are now and what all returns to when this timeful journey is over.

2

MIND THE COMPLICATOR

THE mind is apt to create illusions about the unknown, about what has not been realised or experienced. Expectations and desire are the basis for this. The projections are fabricated out of imagination, out of the written and spoken word, even out of unverifiable experiences as related by others. The more unusual and remarkable they are, the more they draw the mind towards more of the same. Experience has a high standing with the mind. This, it has made its home, one as familiar and as comfortable as an old pair of slippers. Experience greets the mind from its first conscious moment, stays while consciousness functions and fades when consciousness fades. Sleep — any unconscious state — is the verification of this.

Mind doesn't function in a vacuum. Nor does it willingly move towards that which is undesired or not dressed up in appealing fashion. A considerable return, psychological, physical or material is the basis for its actions. So it builds its big picture of what it expects from life through what it does. It is the same when it ventures forth to discover the spiritual.

Outstanding returns are expected in joy, peace, love, harmony; in self-control, in the realisation of the truth about existence, the nature of the universe, even in sharing some of the unusual happenings it hears about. Oh, so much it expects from this most wonderful of journeys.

Mind has fashioned its expectations from what it hears here and there, from books, or speakers who affirm their standing through what they say. To those who are discontented, lost and looking for that something special, the lure is irresistible. More so if there is a supportive group to join with distinctive dress, unorthodox disciplines and perhaps the encouragement to indulge sexually and throw aside old taboos and restraints.

True spiritual development is the result of unrelenting application towards self-understanding. It goes hand in hand with revealing insights into behaviour and the motives that direct the self on its course through life. It enables the mind to disentangle itself from the collective influences that impinge from the outer and the desires, demands and fears that arise inwardly. Any fancy stuff along the way gives a temporary lift at the time.

These happenings are not so rare. Many claim an experience or two. But what happens when these experiences pass if there is no solid basis of spiritual understanding to fall back on? The emptiness, the feeling of being lost or the discontent creeps back in and the desire for more of the unusual takes over again.

The true measure of a spiritual life is reflected in how the ordinary run of experiences, the downturns, the hassles, the difficulties are quietly faced without disturbing the inner balance that spiritual discovery brings.

Looking always for the spectacular, the astonishing or whatever else you hear about in life is like walking the seashore looking for shells. Hear the exclamations of delight when the supposedly valuable and rare comes to light. Is there then no beauty, no wonder in the surroundings when these are absent?

Look again, with full attention at the sand, at the sea, the surf that washes over the sand then recedes, at everything cast up on the shore — seaweed, stones, the occasional dead fish or crab, or wading birds foraging for food — there is wonder in all of this if the attention is open to receive.

Through desire and intention, mind plants its own movement across the face of time. Then it works, thinks and acts to fulfil its intentions. This is the extent of the self — an overlay pouring out, covering the light that shines within.

Archaeology is the science that digs down through strata of accumulation to unearth the foundations of past civilisations beneath the overburden. Likewise, the spiritual seeker must turn, not towards the encouragement of desire to experience the unusual, but inwards, removing layer after layer of covering attitudes until the true essence of what is hidden reveals its nature.

3

THE MIND ABROAD

YOU may have noticed how the search for the spectacular drives many onwards, ever onwards. In movies it is obvious with ingenious effects; in the circus, with ever more death-defying and difficult acts; in the tasks that individuals set themselves, climbing difficult mountains, canoeing down dangerous rapids. Always the mind reaches out to go a step further. The quiet life of contemplation, of self-investigation is not accorded much value. The desire of the self is to stand out on some pinnacle of achievement so it can say, "I have truly lived above and beyond the ordinary." The attraction is there and many worship at its shrine.

The attractions offered by the outer world are obvious. Of the inner, of a journey to the source of what we are, not so obvious. There are no barriers that test us physically, no swift-flowing rapids to navigate nor dangers to test human courage.

Yet nevertheless, certain qualities are necessary. ENDURANCE — to stay the course till the flag of self-discovery is unfurled. DEDICATION — so that we are not distracted from this purpose by wayward desire to wander elsewhere. ATTENTION — that remains firmly focused on uncovering the truth about the nature of the mind, its motives and behavioural patterns. The capacity to reflect consistently on a theme until the solution is clear and a refusal to let the ego interfere and take control for its own sense of self-importance.

We may not be able to do great deeds of derring-do in the outer world but we can all take the high road to the strangeness of our ultimate nature. All it takes is an eager heart to get started.

There is little expense involved in this spiritual undertaking, just a book or two to begin with. The rest — earnestness, eagerness and interest — is supplied free of charge. If a master is not nearby, not to worry. The inner guru is always available and ready to lend a hand at the opportune moment.

The main thing is not to be overawed, to proceed a step at a time to absorb the written expressions that appeal. Pass by on those that are difficult to relate to or do not attract. That may be a sign they are not for you. You may return to them later as understanding deepens. In any case, life in its wisdom has provided something for everyone. Hence the variety of expressions on the open market for the earnest seeker.

Don't try too much at once, whether it is reading, the practice of meditation or the disciplines you decide are conducive to preparing the ground for an eventual spiritual harvest. Habit is a powerful guideline for the mind and perhaps the best way to regulate time, in the early stages of this journey, is through regular routines of time allocated to what you decide on doing.

The purpose of all this preparation is to set the seeds of enquiry below the surface extent, deep within the mind. The intention is to evoke a response from the inner guardian, that deeper awareness that stands silent watch over its human offspring.

Self-effort can only go so far, only do so much. After we've done all we can, we need a helping hand from the inner witness that observes and understands all, yet is ever ready to respond to the genuine seeker who sincerely longs to rejoin the universal source.

The biggest difficulty along the way is the perennial ego, always urging to keep control of the whole show, to have everything revolve within the limited orbit of its own desires and arrangements.

Ego wants to be judge and jury, the centre of attention, the one at the beginning, in the middle and at the end of everything going on. It is the little dictator, strutting on the stage of life, laying out controlling guidelines then going along for the ride to see what wonders lie ahead. With a limited intelligence at the beginning, where else can this lead but to a limited conclusion?

To keep it in hand, Ego must be kept under watchful surveillance at all times. Otherwise it will slip its leash and run riot. And when Ego runs riot, nothing else gets a look in. It's Ego here, Ego there, Ego everywhere in one guise or another. Such a vast repertoire of disguises and such a consummate actor.

Any role, any posture in convincing fashion. The good, the bad and the ugly, in the forefront of every conceivable subterfuge — duty bound in the defence of high ideals, allied to worthy causes, the crusader against evil, the seeker after truth and the highest nature of all — capable of exploiting any situation to its own advantage and, as always, seeking self-establishment,   enhancement, protection for its own little existence and affairs. Wherever it is, whatever it does, it needs careful watching and the wind taken out of its sails to slow down its momentum or it will create merry mayhem. Service to the self is its business and in this, it is a genius indeed. No one can do it better than master or mistress self.

You'll gather from all this that I am not a champion of the self. Let me clarify this. By 'self' I mean the limited, the operating within personal boundaries from a conditioned background whose only interest is to maintain and perpetuate its influence. Whatever the background, Self is locked into this and the thinking and actions that follow are the voice and expression of the background.

Whereas Self that has broken out of these confines to lodge in the Eternal, the unlimited and expansive, takes on the qualities of the Eternal. This, then, becomes the guiding directive of the thinking and behaviour that follows.

Outwardly, this may not be that noticeable but inwardly, the self is constantly cleared of accumulation, free of impediments and the interaction between the Eternal and the human outlet proceeds with little hindrance.

Sounds simple doesn't it? In reality, the clearing of the inner expressway is a devilishly difficult matter for the involved seeker. There is nothing as stubborn as an ego intent on holding onto its own. It takes the power of an ongoing spiritual input to shatter the hold and dissolve the background content the ego relies on for sustenance and substance in its journey through life.

"Why must it let go?" you may ask. "Isn't it nothing without its background, national, social and religious, its input from time?"

Maybe, but this is what isolates it from others with different backgrounds. Contention follows, a battle for supremacy, for economic advantage, and that means war and that means suffering on an expanding scale.

With the background conditioning and its divisive ways rampant there is nothing to weld people together into a harmonious whole — not the understanding, not the love, not the spiritual realisation which is not and never can be a product of the background's conditioning.

It is not different nationalities that come to rest in the one spiritual nature, not separate selves imbued with distinction but that side of each and every human that is of the same nature. Now, you are not going to be convinced by mere words that this is so. You need much more than this. You need self-discovery, a putting aside of everything the self appears to be, all its extensive activities that are time related and allowing the 'other' to shine through and do its own thing, whatever this is.

You will be overjoyed, exhilarated with the consequences. And yes, you will also be surprised and shocked at what you see and learn about yourselves. Self-prejudice in one's favour is a master painter. It is not easy to get past the picture it presents and discover the unbiased truth. But that is one of the gifts that comes your way when realisation and integration take place. There's no telling what may follow but it is all part of the new learning that begins and proceeds to unfold.

4

SELF IS THE PROBLEM

YOU may have gathered from all the foregoing that although the self responds to an inner urging of heart and mind to travel inwards towards the Silent Heart, true action doesn't eventuate until the spiritual intervenes and directs the show like a master maestro conducting an orchestra with super skill. It is rather humiliating somewhere along the way for the ego to realise this. It does have a high opinion of its worth and capacity to produce results through applied effort.

Listen to the reasons it projects wherever it goes, whatever it does. So convincing, isn't it? Logical reasons to explain, to determine, to persuade. There's no end to it. Like a master magician on the stage of life — a wave of the wand of reason and there you have it, unassailable reasons as to the why, what and wherefore of the self's actions.

Look into the motives behind the reasons and there you will uncover the self and its prejudiced standing. Reason is directed to serve the self and that means, in effect, to serve the understanding reflected and the background of influences identified with. Clear this backlog of confusion and the inner light has a chance to come shining through.

And what clears the backlog? Not action from the level of the self which is under its control and acts to preserve its property rights and standing in the community of selves, but integrated action from an alert watchfulness that passively observes the interaction going on.

Mind, in its passively alert state, has a remarkable capacity to expose the motives that shape the self's reactions and guide its thinking. Hidden prejudices, likes and dislikes, the predisposition to pass judgments according to an adopted framework of ideas and concepts of what is right and wrong, false perceptions and misunderstandings that parade as truth. Whatever patterns are active are all brought out into the light of consciousness for the benefit of the self's learning.

This unlocking of the inner, influencing background signifies an awakening spirituality. That's what it's all about, revealing the nature of the self to the self. Self draws its strength to function and behave from its adopted background. Expose the limitations inherent in this, clear it out of the way, flood the inner with the light of a new understanding and the basis is there for an entirely different expression in the world of timeful experience.

Controlled by the conditioned background and personal desires, Self is beset with problems, can't see its way clear to proceed joyfully down the highway of life. With the background dissolved by the light of spiritual understanding, energy is released, an inner effervescence takes over, Self goes lightly down the highway and troubles only ruffle the surface. They do not penetrate to disturb the inner serenity that is the spiritual birthright of all.

Having built up a case for the spiritual as far as words can do this, what now? Self wants guidelines, the means and the ways to take itself there or wherever it is that Self without enlightened understanding posits the spiritual. Again, find what you are comfortable with — the books, the meditation techniques, the nature retreats, the religion or movement you are drawn to. You'll do this anyway. No one will stay long with what feels uncomfortable. All this preparation is only the beginning and signifies the intention to devote one's self to reaching out for something better to live by. Perception must be cultivated to appreciate what has true value rather than spurious worth.

The outer does not corrupt unless the person is capable of being corrupted. We cannot be led astray when the inner light is shining brightly. Be prepared for heartache, for rough sailing, for mistakes aplenty. There is important learning in all this. What we do outwardly, the situations that arise, are a reflection of the fears, of what we hold to inwardly and of our need to learn. Challenges and relationships draw out our innermost thoughts and feelings. Be alert, observe and you will learn. Deep interest and attention will reveal your story, its full content.

Do not become too deeply enmeshed in ways and means, no matter how supportive. Break the habitual patterns from time to time to see how you feel and what kind of hold they have developed on you. They can become tunnels that restrict the self's vision. This means you've replaced the former conditioning with another just as limiting, even if it is more acceptable.

Self is complex in its movements. Its story is unravelled a little at a time. Its capacity to change direction, to re-establish itself in different directions and patterns is remarkable in its scope and versatility. It can only be brought to heel with its capacity to do damage removed by a continuing spiritual input.

Intellectually, all manner of interpretations are given to the words depending on the understanding of the reader, but the ongoing reality of what the words are trying to convey is only experienced from moment to moment when the Universal Oneness enfolds the self into the nature that *it is*.

A dynamic release follows — not only joyful. Pleasurable as this is, it is the clear-view seeing, the insights released, the raised awareness that has the greater value with effects that are longer lasting than a burst of joy. Seeing truly, directly, into the nature of the self is intensely liberating. You'll be up in the clouds while it lasts, looking down from up high at what was formerly the self you took yourself to be. This struggling, little movement so full of its own importance, so often locked into frustration and disappointments, is seen to be merely bubbles on the surface of consciousness; just a meandering river of effort reaching out to be other than what it is, like a musical instrument wanting to be the whole orchestra.

Much has been said and written about the self, of how it should be put aside to discover the universal side of existence. But it is a stubborn movement for all that. Explanations, books full of words do not cover what the self is and how it functions. The lifetime of the self is a constantly changing story with intricate plots and subplots. Each individual story is different from another. In a way, it has two authors — one, the surface one, identified with the central actor, the body of flesh, and the other, a witnessing one that watches over the antics of the other. Words, explanations, give an indication of what is going on but the reality of it has to be lived and fully experienced to know and understand it as it is.

Remaining on the level of intellectual appreciation tells you only so much. The conclusions are reasonable ones. Feelings tell you what feelings can. They cannot take you any further. The full story of the self, as it unfolds from day to day, is only understood from the higher level of the witnessing awareness. Living down in valleys you have only a limited view of the terrain. From the top of a high mountain, the view is more extensive.

Change the standpoint from that of the little self to the witnessing one and you are in a position to clearly understand the intricate responses of the self. And you also see what you couldn't see before — how the self is responsible for much of its troubles and the nature of what is meant by the word 'limited' in reference to the self. You also go beyond the word, the variable meanings words have, and get to what the words represent.

Self is not a fixture. Much of what takes place simmers underground, out of sight, like the pressures below in a dormant volcano.

You never know when it's going to blow its top or what kind of reaction, outburst or moods are going to flow out. A surface viewpoint is far too inflexible, too anchored in the pictures it is accustomed to, to keep up with what goes on below the surface.

Reasonable introspection gives a clue but it needs a shift from the separative and surface standing to one that is not limited by this typical approach if the self is to see clearly into the internal workings of its own movement. Whichever way you look at it, Self is the mainspring of the human approach to life.

Understanding what goes on behind the label is very important. The deeper the understanding, the happier the expression — the shallower, well, you have a centre of contention abroad in time.

Anchored in the self in the usual way, dominated by a thinking process that presents a limited and fixed view of how things are, unmindful of its relationship with the universal, the human expression runs riot doing what it will. Clash, counter clash, confusion, contention, divisions and disagreements are the consequences of a limited approach to life and relationships.

To encourage people out of this standpoint, to urge them to reach out for the universal and gain the blessings this higher nature brings is a somewhat daunting undertaking. It is made so by the inadequacies of language and the difference between the understanding that flows out and the understanding that listens.

Interpretation is the reaction of the unrealised self. Not having the reality of the spiritual, Self falls back on reason to clear its confusion. This can be logically convincing and the self is persuaded that it understands the issues, whereas in reality, nothing of spiritual value has come its way. All it has are convincing reasonable conclusions. Through this it does not shift from the field of the mind, from everything it knows. Spiritual transformation isn't effected and infallible evidence of its spiritual connection is absent.

Although reason has a role to play, a spiritual awakening is not primarily an intellectual exploration of questions and answers. This is the language the mind understands, the only one, so it is not entirely discarded. But the constant use of the intellect via the spearhead of reasonable introspection and analysis keeps the sense of separation alive. In this, what hope is there for the realisation of the One, while the many are in ascendance?

Self-abnegation is a difficult art. So many strands of the self are in movement urging for expression. The momentum towards space, time and experience is powerful and insistent. It is hard to put the brakes on and shift the focus of attention to the timeless. Since the timeless has no definable characteristics, Self is at a loss as to how to proceed.

Until the self pushes itself to the limits of what it is capable of and comes to the realisation that it has gone as far as it is capable of going and so comes to a deep standstill, the culmination in this business of self-discovery cannot unfold.

In the moment of deep silence that follows the letting go of all self-movement, the unexpected happens. Subject merges with object, separation fades and the unexplainable, the incomprehensible is there. The timeless is abroad and the limited self has vanished for a moment. The heartfelt longings of the self, the written expressions absorbed along the way, reasonable reflection, meditation, discussion, everything set in motion has come to fruition in this moment of silence with the dawning of the universal light. And the aftermath? A vibrant and energetic expression returns to time, eager to get on with the learning and to take it as far as it can go. One taste is enough to have the self hungry for more until its return to the spiritual source is as complete as it can be. And rest assured that is where the heart will stay, regardless of the meanderings of a restless mind.

5

CONCLUSION

SO, what do I value most now after 40 years of spiritual journeying? Not the unusual happenings, although there has been a share of these. In the early phases, after the initial breakthrough to what I refer to as a spiritual dimension, at times of experiencing joyous outbursts I would find myself visited by spiritual beings in human form. They were aware of my presence as I was of theirs. They dropped in like friends who knew they were welcome. There was nothing imaginative about them. Their presences were distinct. They were such a light-hearted delightful lot, always smiling and they seemed to reflect pleasure in my new-found joy.

There was no attempt at communication. To me they were light beings in tune with the timeless beyond, with the power to appear when and where they chose. Thinking, intellectual intensity such as we express, did not appear to be part of their nature.

They were my happy companions and they offered support with their presence and encouragement to my spiritual aspirations. They only dropped in occasionally but such was their quality that often, when I was gloomy, I longed to be amongst their kind, so gentle, so carefree and light were they.

One night, during a particularly down period, I sat to meditate and soon drifted inwards into quietness. A scene opened out. Two of these beings were beside a stream. I seemingly floated down towards them.

One smiled at the other and said, "Look, here comes Joe."

As I neared, I was suddenly confronted by a man, considerably aged. He remonstrated with me, pointed sternly back in the direction I came from and indicated quite bluntly that my business was back with my own kind.

That was the end of my interaction with these delightful

presences. I would love to share more time with them if I could, communicate in our way if possible and learn more about them.

Even more interesting was the advanced spiritual being I named The Lady of the Light. She first appeared at a time when I was struggling and somewhat despondent. I was sitting on my bed at the time and suddenly she was there, as plain as any person could be. She didn't speak, nor did she have to.

She communicated without words and the meaning was clear: "With all you have, why do you fuss so?" That's all, then she was gone.

There was the presence of a very aged man behind her at the time but he didn't take such a forward role.

She made several more appearances over the years. Now, she too has faded out of my life, visibly that is, though I have no doubt that on the level she has her being, she is in touch with more than myself.

So there have been unusual happenings along the way, even insights into world affairs that proved to be surprisingly accurate. There were also some big boo-boos and these served to curb my youthful arrogance and know-it-all attitude that developed early on. It is easy to get big headed, but life has its way of cutting you down to size and, to declare confidently that something is going to happen and then find that it doesn't is a good lesson in humility.

One of the more precise events that came to light set a timeframe at the turn of the century. As I saw it, a suffering mankind, worldwide, eyes filled with tears, began to take the first positive footsteps in a new direction.

I understood this to mean a movement back to the spiritual source and a turning away from the past disruptive and self-centred ways. What kind of pressures or turmoil will bring mankind to this point I wasn't shown. I hope it's not too painful. Surely there's been enough thus far in this century. I may yet be around to see how it turns out.

Still, enough of the unusual. What do I value most? That is hard to define. I'm much more alive and aware inwardly. The ways of the self, its intellectual intensity are carried lightly now. The meandering ways of the mind, of desires, do not build up into forceful movements that take over. There has been a shift from being caught up in polarities and concepts.

I drift along a placid stream. Turmoil may be around me but inwardly there is calm. Unfortunately I cannot take you with me beyond the words and images so you can experience all this for yourselves.

It is your business what you do with your lives. Whether words stir you to make your own movement towards what is real or whether you prefer to continue to dedicate yourselves only to life in the fast, troubled lane of appearance is up to you.

Much of a spiritual journey is fun. No doubt, if you go and make it to "THAT" which fulfils in its own way, you too may have an interesting story to tell. There are difficulties along the way. Sleepy times are not learning times.

But what comes your way, what opens out, enriches living in so many ways — in warmth, in contentment, in deeper, more sensitive relationships with your partner, friends and family, the people you meet.

What you deeply feel, what you learn will mostly be beyond the capacity of words and reason to communicate. Not much can be done about that.

What matters is, the heart comes to rest in the universal self and that is the beginning of a never-ending love affair that never grows old or tiresome but that is always fresh, new and enchanting. And it colours outer life and relationships in the same fashion.

So go there and join a celestial party. Be one of the happy people who sing the praises of the Spiritual Strangeness. Turn away from the darkness of the mind. Face the sunshine of life. Bask in its glow.

Replenish and refresh yourselves at this universal source. Drink your fill, then go out in the world and share what you can with your brothers and sisters lost in time. Give out the love that has been freely given to you and make this earth a happier place. God knows, it needs it. Good luck and God bless you.

Joseph Raffa. 14 June 1995.

About the author

JOSEPH RAFFA WAS born in 1927 in Fremantle, Western Australia. He enjoyed an idyllic childhood roaming the bush and the seashore. In his teens Joseph became a dedicated atheist, looking to science for answers to the riddles of life and the universe. Then, in his early twenties, he experienced a moment of discovery that transformed his life. As Joseph's life opened out spiritually following this awakening, he was inspired to put pen to paper to encourage others to embark on their own journey of discovery.

Joseph died of cancer in 2010, leaving behind a legacy of inspirational writing which is now being made available to a wider audience.

For more information about Joseph and his books visit www.towardsthesilentheart.com

Other books by Joseph Raffa

Beside Still Waters

ISBN 9780987227676

This beautiful collection of essays touches on the universal search for meaning and inspires readers to reach out for the still waters of the spirit.

The human heart longs for peace and harmony. It seeks a restful haven from the relentless busyness of everyday life, drawing us to spend tranquil moments in natural surrounds that offer a brief respite from the hustle and bustle. There is a state of inner stillness, when the endless chatter of the mind has ceased, that a deeper understanding arises. These are the 'still waters' that bring new life to mankind, that lay claim to the heart and redirect the mind. These are the waters of peace, love and true togetherness that lift us up to divine heights of being and living.

The Silent Guardian

ISBN 9780987227669

A timely reminder of our spiritual journey and true purpose on Earth.

Joseph shares an inspirational message for those who care to listen.

'Explore the planets, the outer reaches of space, the depths of the seas. Burrow into the earth, climb every mountain. When you have seen it all, you will still be left with the mystery of yourself. Turn and face this. Explore this. When you've travelled the extent and depth of the human expression, much of what you learn will be beyond the mind's capacity to convey through verbalisation. When heart speaks to heart, what more is there to say?'

The Silent Guardian

Beyond the Cross

The Christ Collection

ISBN 9780987227652

A moving collection of inspired pieces about Jesus.

Joseph Raffa was a dedicated atheist when he set out in search of answers to the riddles of life and the universe. Then, in a blissful moment of discovery, the God the Bible speaks of, the Allah of Mohammed and the longed for Nirvana of the Buddhists came into his life. As his life opened out spiritually, Joseph began to have a deeper appreciation of Jesus, His life and His role in the spiritual awakening of Mankind. Visions and insights arose unbidden, in such a manner that their authenticity could not be questioned. The young man who was an atheist for a time, who cared not to read the Bible or take much notice of Christ and His life, found himself anchored in God and also writing pieces extolling the virtues, the wisdom and the love expressed by that super spiritual being of long ago.

Thank you for taking the time to read this book. Ratings and reviews are appreciated. If you enjoyed it, please Tweet/Share on your social media networks.